SAGITTARIUS: (NOVEMBER 22 - DECEMBER 21)

The Archer's Quest Adventure and Wisdom in the Fire of Sagittarius. THE ASTROLOGY IN OUR PERSONALITIES. The Key To Unlocking The Wonders In Us

Norris Elliott

NORRIS ELLIOTT BOOKS/ELLIONAIRE BOOKS

Copyright © 2023 Norris Elliott

All rights reserved

All rights reserved. No part of this publication may be reproduced, distributed, or transmitted in any form or by any means, including photocopying, recording, or other electronic or mechanical methods, without the prior written permission of the author, except in the case of brief quotations embodied in critical reviews and certain other noncommercial uses permitted by copyright law.

This book is not a work of fiction. However, Names, characters, places, and events are the product of the author's imagination or are used fictitiously. Any resemblance to actual persons, living or dead, events, or locales is entirely coincidental.

First Edition

ISBN

Cover design by: Norris Elliott
Library of Congress Control Number:
Printed in the United States of America

DEDICATION

To the stargazers and soul searchers, the dreamers and the doers, this celestial compendium is dedicated to you. May the wisdom of the stars illuminate your path, guiding you through life's myriad journeys with the light of understanding and the warmth of compassion. Let each page remind you of the interconnectedness of all things, the beauty of our differences, and the shared quest for meaning that unites us under the vast, starlit sky. Here's to the adventures that await, the discoveries to be made, and the endless exploration of the cosmos within and around us. May you find in these words a reflection of your own light and the courage to shine it brightly in the world. .

"Beneath the endless canopy of stars, where the arrow of the Archer points beyond the seen to the unseen, there lies a path paved with the quest for truth and the fire of discovery. Here, in the vast expanse of possibility, Sagittarius teaches us that the journey itself is the destination, and that freedom is found not in arrival, but in the perpetual pursuit of horizons that stretch the soul and ignite the imagination."

ELLIONAIRE

CONTENTS

Title Page
Copyright
Dedication
Epigraph
Author's Foreword

BOOK 9: Sagittarius: (November 22 - December 21)The Archer's Quest	1
Introduction	2
The Sagittarius Child	4
The Sagittarius Youth	6
The Sagittarius Adult	8
The Sagittarius Parent	10
The Sagittarius Partner	12
Sagittarius Luck and Fortune	14
Sagittarius Health and Wellness	16
Sagittarius Strengths and Weaknesses	19
Sagittarius Love and Relationships	21
Famous Sagittarians	23
The Sagittarian Boss:	25
The Sagittarian Worker:	26
The Sagittarian Business Partner	27

Conclusion	28
Appendices	30
Epilogue	31
Sagittarius Themed Quiz	33
Dear Sagittarius Readers,	36
Books By This Author	39

AUTHOR'S FOREWORD

As the author of "Sagittarius: (November 22 - December 21): The Archer's Quest Adventure and Wisdom in the Fire of Sagittarius," my journey into the heart of Sagittarius has been an expedition of its own—a voyage into understanding the boundless enthusiasm, the thirst for knowledge, and the unwavering optimism that characterize those born under this sign. While not a Sagittarius myself, this exploration has allowed me to view the world through the eyes of the Archer, embracing a perspective filled with possibilities and a desire to discover the truths of the universe.

Crafting this narrative required me to channel the Sagittarian spirit of adventure and exploration, to capture the essence of a sign driven by a quest for meaning and a love for the journey itself. It was an exercise in stretching my own boundaries, in learning to appreciate the value of looking beyond the immediate to the vast expanse of the horizon that defines the Sagittarian outlook.

This book aims to serve as a compass for Sagittarians, guiding them through the exploration of their own nature, while also offering insights to those who journey alongside them—friends, lovers, and companions intrigued by the Archer's dynamic energy and philosophical mind. It is a celebration of the fire that propels Sagittarius forward, the arrow that points toward the future, and the unquenchable curiosity that fuels their journey through life.

To the Sagittarians, may you find within these pages a reflection of your own zest for life, a reaffirmation of your quest for knowledge, and a deeper understanding of the freedom you so cherish. May this book inspire you to continue aiming your arrows high, exploring the unknown, and embracing the journey with an open heart and an eager mind.

To those who love and cherish a Sagittarius, may this exploration provide you with a window into the soul of the Archer, offering a glimpse of the world through their eyes—a world where every horizon is a new beginning, every challenge an adventure, and every moment an opportunity to learn, grow, and explore.

Writing "Sagittarius: (November 22 - December 21): The Archer's Quest Adventure and Wisdom in the Fire of Sagittarius " has been a journey of discovery, not just into the essence of Sagittarius but into the broader human experience of seeking, questioning, and aspiring. It is my hope that this book serves as a reminder that, regardless of our astrological signs, we all share the universal desire to understand our place in the cosmos and to pursue our paths with passion and purpose.

With respect and admiration for the Sagittarian spirit,
Norris Elliott

BOOK 9: SAGITTARIUS: (NOVEMBER 22 - DECEMBER 21) THE ARCHER'S QUEST

Adventure and Wisdom in the Fire of Sagittarius

INTRODUCTION

Adventure and Wisdom in the Fire of Sagittarius

Welcome to the vibrant journey of Sagittarius, "The Archer's Quest," where the essence of adventure, wisdom, and the pursuit of truth lights the path. Ruled by Jupiter, the planet of expansion, fortune, and knowledge, Sagittarians embody the spirit of the explorer, the philosopher, and the eternal student of life's mysteries. Their fire sign nature ignites a passion for discovery, an insatiable curiosity, and an optimistic outlook that sees every moment as an opportunity for growth and joy.

Fiery Spirit and Love of Freedom

Sagittarians are driven by a fiery spirit that craves freedom and the space to roam. This love of freedom manifests not just in physical journeys across the globe but also in the exploration of ideas, cultures, and philosophies. Sagittarians seek to expand their horizons in every possible way, driven by the belief that life is an adventure to be embraced with open arms and a fearless heart.

Quest for Knowledge

The Archer's quest is as much about acquiring wisdom as it is about experiencing the thrill of adventure. Sagittarians are perpetual seekers of knowledge, always aiming their arrows toward higher learning, spiritual exploration, and the uncovering of universal truths. Their philosophical nature prompts deep questions and a broad-minded approach to life's complexities, making them avid learners and teachers.

Optimistic Outlook on Life

One of Sagittarius's most endearing qualities is their unshakeable optimism. Governed by Jupiter, they possess a natural ability to see the silver lining in every cloud and to approach life's challenges with humor and grace. This optimism is contagious, inspiring those around them to view the world through a lens of hope and possibility.

Desire for Expansion

Sagittarians are driven by an inherent desire for expansion—in thought, experience, and spirit. They resist being confined to the familiar, constantly pushing the boundaries of their understanding and experience. This desire for growth fuels their adventurous nature, leading them on quests that are as much about internal discovery as they are about external exploration.

The Joy of Discovery

Above all, Sagittarians find joy in the act of discovery. Whether uncovering a hidden gem on their travels, connecting the dots of a complex philosophical theory, or experiencing a spiritual awakening, the joy of finding something new and enlightening is what keeps the Archer's arrow aimed toward the unknown.

As we embark on "The Archer's Quest," we are invited to join Sagittarius on their journey of exploration, wisdom, and boundless optimism. In the fire of Sagittarius, we find the courage to chase our dreams, the wisdom to seek deeper understanding, and the joy that comes from discovering the vast and beautiful tapestry of life. Sagittarius reminds us that the quest itself is as important as the destination, and that the true adventure lies in the continual pursuit of growth, freedom, and enlightenment.

THE SAGITTARIUS CHILD

The Sagittarius child is a bundle of joy and curiosity, their spirit uncontainably vibrant and their energy seemingly endless. Born under the sign of the Archer, these children are natural explorers, philosophers in the making, and seekers of the broadest horizons. With Jupiter as their ruling planet, their lives are marked by a love for freedom, a quest for knowledge, and an optimistic outlook that lights up their path of discovery.

Characteristics of the Sagittarius Child

Curious and Energetic: The Sagittarius child's curiosity knows no bounds. They are the ones with a million questions about everything under the sun, driven by an insatiable desire to understand the world around them. This curiosity, coupled with their boundless energy, often leads them into new and exciting adventures, making every day a chance to learn and explore something new.

Adventurous Spirit: Sagittarius children thrive on adventure and exploration. They are happiest when given the freedom to explore the world around them, whether it's through travel, reading, or imaginative play. Their adventurous spirit is not just about physical travel but also about exploring ideas, cultures, and philosophies, making them the little philosophers of the zodiac.

Nurturing the Sagittarius Child

Encouraging Exploration: To nurture a Sagittarius child's explorative spirit, provide them with opportunities to learn and discover. This could be through books, educational toys, outdoor adventures, or travel. Encourage their questions and help them find the answers, fostering a love for learning that will last a lifetime.

Teaching the Value of Focus and Commitment: While their love for exploration is one of their greatest strengths, Sagittarius children might find it challenging to focus on one task or commit to long-term projects. Teaching them the value of focus and commitment is crucial. This can be done through activities that match their interests but require persistence, such as learning a musical instrument, participating in a sport, or committing to a long-term project like building a model or starting a small garden.

Balancing Freedom with Boundaries: Sagittarius children need freedom to explore and grow, but they also need boundaries to learn about safety and responsibility. Finding the right balance between giving them the space to roam and setting limits is key to their development. Teach them about the importance of responsibility and the consequences of their actions in a way that respects their independence but also ensures their safety.

In nurturing the explorative spirit of the Sagittarius child while teaching them the value of focus and commitment, we help them harness their natural zest for life and curiosity in productive and fulfilling ways. By encouraging their adventurous nature and guiding them to understand the importance of perseverance and dedication, we prepare them for a life full of meaningful discoveries and personal growth, true to the spirit of Sagittarius.

THE SAGITTARIUS YOUTH

The Sagittarius teenager embarks on life's journey with an open heart and an insatiable curiosity, characterized by a deep-seated love for freedom and a broad spectrum of interests. Whether boy or girl, their teenage years are a time of exploration, both of the external world and their inner selves. Nurturing their intellectual and spiritual growth requires an understanding of their need for independence, as well as guidance to appreciate the value of the journey itself.

Sagittarius Boy: The Adventurous Seeker

Embracing Interests: The Sagittarius boy is likely to have a wide range of interests, from sports and outdoor adventures to philosophy and foreign cultures. Encourage him to explore these interests fully, providing resources and opportunities that allow him to dive into his passions. This exploration is key to his intellectual and personal growth.

Love for Freedom: The desire for freedom is strong in the Sagittarius boy, manifesting as a need for personal space and autonomy. It's important to respect this need, allowing him the freedom to make his own choices and learn from them, even if it means making mistakes. This freedom is crucial for his development into a responsible and independent adult.

Guidance on the Journey: While he may focus on the destination, it's important to teach the Sagittarius boy to appreciate the journey as well. Help him understand that growth and learning are found in the experiences along the way, not just in achieving a goal. Encouraging reflection and mindfulness can help him find value and joy in the process of becoming.

Sagittarius Girl: The Intellectual Explorer

Embracing Interests: The Sagittarius girl is a natural explorer, with interests that might range from art and literature to science and activism. Support her exploratory spirit by encouraging her to pursue her passions, whether through extracurricular activities, travel, or self-study. Her intellectual growth is intertwined with her ability to explore and question the world around her.

Love for Freedom: Freedom to the Sagittarius girl means the ability to express herself and to explore her identity without constraints. Create an environment where she feels safe to share her thoughts and ideas, and where her independence is nurtured. This sense of freedom is essential for her to develop her unique voice and path.

Guidance on the Journey: The Sagittarius girl may sometimes be so focused on her future aspirations that she overlooks the importance of the present moment. Encourage her to live in the now and to see each experience as an integral step in her journey. Teaching her to celebrate each moment's learning and joy can help her develop a balanced and fulfilling approach to life.

For both Sagittarius boys and girls, the teenage years are a critical period of growth, discovery, and self-expression. By supporting their intellectual and spiritual exploration and guiding them to appreciate the beauty of the journey itself, we help them build a strong foundation for a life filled with adventure, wisdom, and an enduring quest for knowledge.

THE SAGITTARIUS ADULT

Sagittarius adults embark on life's journey with an undiminished thirst for adventure, an enduring love for learning, and a quest for meaningful pursuits that align with their philosophical views. As they navigate the complexities of adulthood, both Sagittarius men and women strive to balance their innate need for independence and freedom with the desire for deep, lasting connections that bring richness and fulfillment to their lives.

Sagittarius Male: The Philosophical Adventurer

Seeking Fulfillment: The Sagittarius man continues to seek fulfillment through exploration, whether it's through travel, engaging with different cultures, or delving into various fields of study. His pursuit of knowledge is not just academic but deeply personal, as he seeks to understand the world and his place within it. Encouraging his exploratory nature while reminding him of the importance of grounding can help him find a balance between his adventurous spirit and the practicalities of life.

Balancing Independence: The Sagittarius man values his independence highly, often seeing it as integral to his identity and personal growth. As he matures, however, he learns that true freedom comes with the ability to form deep, meaningful connections without losing oneself. Guiding him to understand that vulnerability and emotional intimacy can coexist with independence is key to helping him form lasting relationships that do not feel confining but rather enriching.

The Rewards of Connection: Encouraging the Sagittarius man to invest in relationships—be it romantic, friendship, or family—highlights the rewards of deep connections. Sharing adventures, intellectual pursuits, and philosophical discussions with loved ones can bring a new level of fulfillment and joy to his life, showing him that sometimes, the greatest adventures are shared.

Sagittarius Female: The Independent Seeker

Seeking Fulfillment: The Sagittarius woman pursues a life filled with purpose and adventure. Her quest for fulfillment often involves a blend of travel, learning, and the pursuit of causes that resonate with her ethical and philosophical beliefs. Supporting her need for autonomy while encouraging her to find purpose in connections and community can help her achieve a fulfilling balance.

Balancing Independence: Independence is a cornerstone of the Sagittarius woman's life, driving her decisions and shaping her path. Learning to balance this need with the human desire for connection and intimacy can be a journey in itself. Providing her with the space to explore her independence while also emphasizing the beauty of deep emotional bonds can guide her towards fulfilling relationships that respect her freedom.

The Rewards of Connection: The Sagittarius woman thrives in environments where she can share her passions and discoveries with others. Encouraging her to cultivate relationships based on mutual respect, adventure, and intellectual growth can deepen her appreciation for the connections in her life. Showing her that independence and intimacy are not mutually exclusive but rather complementary aspects of a rich, adventurous life can enhance her pursuit of fulfillment.

For both Sagittarius men and women, adulthood is a journey of balancing the wild call of independence with the deep human need for connection. By embracing this balance, they can discover that the most rewarding adventures often come from the shared experiences and the meaningful bonds they forge along the way.

THE SAGITTARIUS PARENT

Parenting as a Sagittarius brings a unique blend of wonder, ethical considerations, and an insatiable quest for knowledge into the familial realm. Whether as a father or mother, Sagittarius parents are keen on nurturing their children's curiosity about the world, instilling a sense of moral integrity, and encouraging the pursuit of wisdom in all its forms. Their challenge lies in balancing their love for freedom and adventure with providing the stable foundation that children need to thrive.

Sagittarius Father: The Adventurous Mentor

Inspiring Wonder and Ethics: The Sagittarius father is naturally inclined to inspire a sense of wonder in his children. He shares stories of his adventures, instills a love for the outdoors, and discusses philosophical and ethical questions, making these conversations a regular part of family life. He's keen on teaching his children to question, to seek truth, and to live by a strong moral compass.

Fostering Exploration: Encouraging his children to be explorers, the Sagittarius father supports their quests for knowledge and self-discovery. He's the first to suggest a family trip to somewhere new or to turn a simple weekend outing into an adventure. He values experiences over material gifts, believing that the best education comes from interacting with the world.

Providing Stability: Balancing his wanderlust with the responsibilities of parenting, the Sagittarius father strives to provide a stable foundation for his children. He understands the importance of consistency and presence in his children's lives and works to blend his adventurous spirit with the demands of parenting, showing his children that stability and freedom can coexist harmoniously.

Sagittarius Mother: The Open-minded Guide

Inspiring Wonder and Ethics: The Sagittarius mother instills a love for learning and ethical living in her children, encouraging them to see the world as a place full of possibilities and lessons. She engages them in conversations about different cultures, religions, and philosophies, teaching them to appreciate diversity and to form their own moral viewpoints.

Fostering Exploration: She champions her children's independence and personal growth, encouraging them to pursue their interests, even if they lead down unconventional paths. The Sagittarius mother is always there to support her children's explorations, whether by providing resources, sharing in their discoveries, or simply listening to their day's adventures with genuine interest.

Providing Stability: While she nurtures their free spirits, the Sagittarius mother also knows the value of a secure home base. She works to create a nurturing environment where her children feel loved and supported, regardless of where their explorations take them. She teaches them that while the world is vast and full of wonders, the love and support of family is a constant they can always rely on.

For Sagittarius parents, the art of parenting is about inspiring their children to dream big, to question, and to explore, all while ensuring that they feel grounded and secure. By fostering open-mindedness, curiosity, and the courage to pursue one's interests, Sagittarius parents prepare their children for a life filled with adventure, learning, and a deep appreciation for the richness of the world around them.

THE SAGITTARIUS PARTNER

In love, Sagittarians, whether male or female, bring a vibrant, explorative spirit to their relationships. Governed by Jupiter, the planet of growth and expansion, they seek partnerships that are built on a foundation of honesty, shared adventures, and philosophical explorations. The key to a fulfilling relationship with a Sagittarius lies in respecting their need for freedom and personal growth, while also deepening the bond through shared experiences and intellectual connection.

Sagittarius Male: The Explorer in Love

Valuing Honesty and Adventure: The Sagittarius man places high value on honesty and openness in his relationships. He seeks a partner who is not just a lover but also a fellow adventurer—someone who shares his thirst for exploration and discovery. Shared adventures, whether traveling to new places, trying out new activities, or engaging in stimulating discussions, form the cornerstone of his romantic relationships.

Philosophical Explorations: A relationship with a Sagittarius man is never shallow. He desires a partner with whom he can explore life's big questions, someone who is not afraid to delve into philosophical and ethical discussions. This intellectual bond is as important to him as the emotional and physical connection, providing a basis for a deep and enduring partnership.

Cultivating Freedom and Growth: The Sagittarius man cherishes his freedom and expects his partner to do the same. However, he understands that a successful relationship involves mutual growth and respect for each other's individual journeys. Encouraging personal development and supporting each other's goals and dreams are essential for keeping the relationship vibrant and fulfilling.

Sagittarius Female: The Adventurous Companion

Valuing Honesty and Adventure: The Sagittarius woman is drawn to relationships that promise honesty, laughter, and a shared sense of adventure. She looks for a partner who is willing to join her on her quest for knowledge and experience, someone who can match her enthusiasm for life and its myriad possibilities. Together, they find joy in the journey, making every day an opportunity for new discoveries.

Philosophical Explorations: Intellectual compatibility is crucial for the Sagittarius woman. She seeks a partner who is curious about the world, open to exploring different viewpoints, and willing to engage in deep conversations about life, the universe, and everything in between. This shared pursuit of wisdom strengthens their bond and enriches their relationship.

Cultivating Freedom and Growth: For the Sagittarius woman, a relationship must nurture her independence and allow her the space to grow. She values a partner who respects her need for freedom and supports her personal development, just as she does theirs. A successful relationship with a Sagittarius woman is one where both partners are free to explore their individual paths, knowing that their journeys are intertwined.

For Sagittarians, male or female, love is an adventure that is best shared with a partner who values honesty, cherishes freedom, and is open to exploring all that life has to offer. Cultivating a relationship that respects the need for personal space and growth, while also deepening the connection through shared experiences and intellectual explorations, can lead to a dynamic and enduring partnership.

SAGITTARIUS LUCK AND FORTUNE

Sagittarius, the sign of the Archer, is blessed with a natural inclination towards optimism, adventure, and a desire for expansion, traits that are closely tied to the influence of their ruling planet, Jupiter. This beneficent giant of the solar system brings luck, growth, and an ever-broadening perspective on life. By understanding and embracing their lucky elements, Sagittarians can further capitalize on their innate characteristics and navigate their path with even greater fortune.

Sagittarius's Lucky Elements

Colors: Sagittarians find luck in the rich and vibrant shades of purple and blue. These colors resonate with their expansive nature and philosophical mindset, encouraging wisdom, prosperity, and higher thought processes.

Numbers: 3, 7, and 9 are considered lucky numbers for Sagittarius, each embodying an aspect of their adventurous spirit and love for exploration. These numbers often signal new opportunities for growth and expansion in various aspects of their lives.

Gemstones: Turquoise and topaz are gemstones that bring luck to Sagittarians. Turquoise is known for its protective and healing properties, enhancing communication and intuition, while topaz stimulates Sagittarius's optimistic nature, attracting abundance and good fortune.

Days: Thursday, ruled by Jupiter, is a particularly auspicious day for Sagittarians. Engaging in new ventures, long-term planning, or philosophical studies on this day can be especially fruitful.

Capitalizing on Optimism and Desire for Expansion

Sagittarians' innate optimism is a powerful magnet for attracting positive outcomes and opportunities. By maintaining a positive outlook and being open to new experiences, they can often find themselves in the right place at the right time. Their desire for expansion, both intellectually and geographically, propels them into adventures that enrich their lives and broaden their horizons.

The Influence of Jupiter Transits

Jupiter transits are significant periods for Sagittarians, offering enhanced opportunities for growth, learning, and exploration. These transits often bring about a deepening of philosophical understanding and an increased appetite for adventure. Sagittarians can make the most of these periods by:

- **Seeking Knowledge:** Jupiter's influence makes it an ideal time to pursue higher education, engage in spiritual or philosophical studies, or explore new cultures and ideas.
- **Expanding Horizons:** Whether through travel, taking up new hobbies, or expanding their social circle, Sagittarians should embrace the opportunities to broaden their life experience.
- **Reflecting and Planning:** Use the optimistic and expansive energy of Jupiter to reflect on personal goals and to plan for future endeavors. Setting intentions during this period can lead to significant achievements and fulfillment.

By understanding their lucky elements and harnessing the optimistic and expansive energy of Jupiter, Sagittarians can further enrich their journey through life. The influence of Jupiter transits is a time of enhanced fortune and opportunity, encouraging Sagittarians to explore, grow, and embrace the boundless possibilities that life offers.

SAGITTARIUS HEALTH AND WELLNESS

For Sagittarius, the sign synonymous with exploration and freedom, maintaining health and wellness involves a dynamic blend of physical activity, outdoor adventures, and pursuits that nourish the mind and spirit. Governed by Jupiter, Sagittarians possess a natural enthusiasm for life that, when channeled into healthful practices, can significantly enhance their overall well-being.

Physical Health: The Call of the Outdoors

Physical Activity: Sagittarians thrive on movement and have an innate need for physical activity that challenges and engages them. Activities such as hiking, horseback riding, archery, or any sport that allows them to stretch their legs and explore the outdoors are particularly beneficial. Regular exercise not only keeps them physically fit but also satisfies their craving for adventure.

Outdoor Adventures: The great outdoors is Sagittarius's gym, playground, and meditation space all rolled into one. Spending time in nature—whether it's a walk in the park, a camping trip, or an adventurous trek—recharges their batteries and keeps them grounded. The connection to nature supports their physical health by reducing stress, enhancing mood, and providing a natural setting for physical activity.

Mental Wellness: The Pursuit of Meaning

Meaningful Pursuits: Sagittarians possess a deep-seated need to find meaning and purpose in their lives. Engaging in pursuits that align with their personal philosophy and broaden their horizons

SAGITTARIUS: (NOVEMBER 22 - DECEMBER 21)

supports their mental wellness. This could involve travel, learning new languages, philosophical studies, or volunteer work. Pursuits that combine physical activity with intellectual or spiritual growth, such as yoga or martial arts, are especially rewarding for them.

Connections: While fiercely independent, Sagittarians also benefit from meaningful connections with others who share their zest for life and quest for knowledge. Maintaining relationships with friends and family, and being part of communities that share their interests, can provide emotional support and a sense of belonging. Social interactions, especially those that involve learning or exploring new ideas, are vital for their mental wellness.

Strategies for Well-being

1. **Routine Flexibility:** Incorporate a variety of physical activities into their routine to keep exercise interesting and engaging. Flexibility in their schedule allows for spontaneous adventures, satisfying their need for freedom.
2. **Mindfulness Practices:** Meditation, mindfulness, or journaling can help Sagittarians stay present and grounded, balancing their expansive nature with a sense of inner calm.
3. **Goal Setting:** Encourage setting achievable goals related to physical health, intellectual pursuits, and personal growth. This provides direction for their adventurous spirit and a sense of accomplishment when goals are met.
4. **Community Engagement:** Participating in group activities, clubs, or classes that align with their interests can provide both social and intellectual stimulation, enhancing their sense of well-being.

By focusing on a balanced approach that caters to both their physical need for activity and their mental need for meaningful engagement, Sagittarians can maintain optimal health and wellness. Embracing the outdoors, pursuing interests that fulfill them, and cultivating connections that enrich their lives are key to the well-being of this free-spirited zodiac sign.

SAGITTARIUS STRENGTHS AND WEAKNESSES

Strengths and Weaknesses of Sagittarius

Embracing the Adventurous Spirit: Sagittarians are known for their adventurous and explorative nature. Their enthusiasm for life and constant quest for knowledge and new experiences are among their greatest strengths. This innate curiosity not only makes them lifelong learners but also gives them a broad perspective on life and its myriad possibilities.

Addressing Restlessness and Tactlessness: However, their love for freedom and adventure can sometimes manifest as restlessness, making it challenging for them to stick to routines or commit to long-term plans. Moreover, their straightforwardness and love for honesty, while admirable, can sometimes cross into tactlessness, potentially hurting others with their bluntness.

Encouraging Mindfulness: Practicing mindfulness can help Sagittarians become more aware of the present moment, reducing their tendency toward restlessness. Mindfulness exercises can teach them to appreciate the here and now, rather than always looking for the next big adventure.

Cultivating Patience and Empathy: Learning to cultivate patience can help Sagittarians with their tendency to seek instant gratification. Through patience, they can understand that some of the best things in life require time to unfold. Developing empathy can also soften their blunt communication style, helping them convey their truth in ways that are considerate of others' feelings.

Friendship with Sagittarius

Open, Honest, and Adventurous: Sagittarian friendships are characterized by openness and honesty. Sagittarians value friends who are not only companions in adventure but also confidants with whom they can share their deepest thoughts. Their friendships often form in the midst of shared adventures and experiences, creating bonds that are both exhilarating and intellectually stimulating.

Celebrating Freedom and Mutual Respect: Sagittarians cherish their independence and respect the same in their friends. They thrive in friendships that celebrate freedom and individuality, where each person supports the other's personal growth and exploration. This mutual respect for individual paths fosters a healthy dynamic where friends feel valued and understood.

Building and Maintaining Friendships: To build and maintain friendships, Sagittarians should focus on nurturing their connections through regular communication and shared experiences. While they love the thrill of meeting new people, deepening existing friendships requires effort and consistency. Planning regular adventures or intellectual explorations can keep the friendship vibrant and engaging.

Respecting Boundaries: Understanding and respecting each other's boundaries is key in Sagittarian friendships. Open discussions about needs and expectations can help ensure that both friends feel free yet connected, allowing the friendship to flourish without feeling restrictive.

In embracing their strengths and addressing their weaknesses, Sagittarians can enhance their adventurous spirit with mindfulness, patience, and empathy, enriching their interactions and relationships. In friendship, their openness, honesty, and love for freedom form the foundation of lasting bonds that are both liberating and deeply fulfilling.

SAGITTARIUS LOVE AND RELATIONSHIPS

Sagittarius, irrespective of gender, approaches love and relationships with an expansive vision that combines the thrill of romance with the quest for shared adventure and growth. Their ideal partner is not just a lover but a fellow traveler on life's journey, someone who shares their thirst for knowledge, their passion for exploration, and their unwavering optimism. In cultivating relationships, Sagittarians seek to create an environment where both partners can grow, understand each other deeply, and provide unwavering support.

Sagittarius Male: The Companion Explorer

Approach to Relationships: The Sagittarius man looks for a partner who resonates with his adventurous spirit and intellectual curiosity. He values freedom and honesty in relationships and seeks someone who is not only independent but also eager to share in his explorations and adventures. His approach to love is open-hearted and generous, with a desire to experience all that life has to offer, together with his partner.

Fostering Mutual Growth: For the Sagittarius man, a relationship must be a journey of mutual growth and discovery. He encourages his partner to pursue their dreams and interests, just as he seeks to explore his own. This shared path of personal development and exploration is crucial for keeping the relationship vibrant and fulfilling.

Understanding and Support: Communication and understanding are key for the Sagittarius man. He seeks a partner who is not only a romantic companion but also a friend with whom he can share his deepest thoughts and dreams. Providing a space where both partners feel heard and supported, especially in their moments of wanderlust or philosophical inquiry, strengthens their bond.

Sagittarius Female: The Adventurous Partner

Approach to Relationships: The Sagittarius woman cherishes freedom and honesty in her relationships. She seeks a partner who is as enthusiastic about life's adventures as she is—someone who appreciates her independence and shares her zest for exploration. Her approach to love is characterized by a desire for a deep and meaningful connection, where both partners inspire and challenge each other to grow.

Fostering Mutual Growth: A relationship with a Sagittarius woman is one of mutual encouragement and support. She values a partnership where both individuals can grow independently and together, exploring their passions and supporting each other's endeavors. This dynamic of shared growth and exploration is essential for the relationship to thrive.

Understanding and Support: For the Sagittarius woman, finding a partner who understands her need for adventure and intellectual stimulation is crucial. She seeks someone who is not only her lover but also her confidant and co-adventurer. Creating a relationship based on deep understanding, mutual respect, and emotional support allows her to feel connected and valued.

In love and relationships, both Sagittarius men and women strive for a partnership that embodies freedom, adventure, and growth. By fostering an environment of mutual understanding, support, and shared exploration, Sagittarians can build lasting relationships that are as enriching and expansive as they are themselves. This approach to love ensures that the relationship remains a journey of discovery, filled with love, laughter, and the joy of shared adventures.

FAMOUS SAGITTARIANS

Sagittarians are celebrated for their adventurous spirit, philosophical insights, and boundless enthusiasm, traits that have propelled many born under this sign to leave a significant mark on the world. Their quest for knowledge, combined with a fearless approach to life, has made Sagittarians influential figures in various domains. Here are a few notable Sagittarians whose contributions reflect the quintessential qualities of this zodiac sign:

Bruce Lee (November 27, 1940)
A martial artist, actor, and philosopher, Bruce Lee's innovative approach to martial arts and his profound philosophical insights revolutionized the way the world views martial arts and physical fitness. His dedication to personal growth and self-expression embodies the Sagittarian pursuit of excellence and exploration.

Mark Twain (November 30, 1835)
Renowned American author and humorist, Mark Twain's wit, wisdom, and critical eye made him one of the most beloved figures in literature. His adventurous spirit and insightful observations on human nature and society are hallmarks of the Sagittarian love for exploration, both geographically and intellectually.

Jane Austen (December 16, 1775)
Although often considered a Capricorn due to her mid-December birthday, Jane Austen's work and life exhibit many qualities associated with Sagittarius, including a sharp wit, a keen understanding of human psychology, and an exploration of societal norms. Her novels continue to be celebrated for their depth, humor, and insightful commentary on the human condition.

Taylor Swift (December 13, 1989)

An iconic singer-songwriter known for her narrative songwriting, Taylor Swift has captivated audiences worldwide with her musical talent and emotional depth. Her adventurous career, marked by genre exploration and heartfelt storytelling, showcases the Sagittarian spirit of growth and self-expression.

Noam Chomsky (December 7, 1928)

A philosopher, cognitive scientist, and political activist, Noam Chomsky's groundbreaking work in linguistics and his unflinching critique of political systems reflect the Sagittarian pursuit of truth and justice. His contributions to intellectual discourse and social activism highlight the sign's commitment to philosophical exploration and societal improvement.

Steven Spielberg (December 18, 1946)

One of the most influential filmmakers in the history of cinema, Steven Spielberg's imaginative storytelling and pioneering spirit have transformed the film industry. His expansive vision and ability to capture the human experience through film embody the Sagittarian traits of adventure, creativity, and exploration.

These notable Sagittarians, through their various contributions, illustrate the rich tapestry of qualities associated with the sign of the Archer. Their lives and work celebrate the adventurous spirit, intellectual curiosity, and enthusiastic approach to life that define Sagittarius, inspiring others to explore, dream, and reach for their highest ideals.

THE SAGITTARIAN BOSS:

The Visionary Leader

Leadership Style: Sagittarian bosses are known for their visionary approach and inspirational leadership. They possess a natural ability to see the big picture and to motivate their team with their enthusiasm and optimism. A Sagittarian boss values freedom, honesty, and intellectual growth, creating a workplace that encourages innovation and exploration.
Empowering the Team: They empower their team by encouraging independent thinking and offering opportunities for personal and professional development. Sagittarian bosses are more like mentors, fostering a supportive environment where creativity and risk-taking are rewarded.
Challenges and Growth: The challenge for a Sagittarian boss often lies in their aversion to detail and routine, which can sometimes lead to overlooking practical aspects of managing a team or project. Encouraging a balanced approach that combines visionary planning with attention to detail can enhance their effectiveness as leaders.

THE SAGITTARIAN WORKER:

The Enthusiastic Innovator

Work Ethic: Sagittarian workers are dynamic, enthusiastic, and always eager to learn. They thrive in environments that offer variety and challenges, bringing a sense of adventure to their work. Their optimistic outlook and adaptability make them valuable team members, capable of inspiring others with their vision and dedication.

Valuing Independence: Independence is crucial for Sagittarian workers. They perform best when given autonomy over their projects and the freedom to explore innovative solutions. Structured flexibility, allowing them to manage their tasks while exploring new ideas, maximizes their productivity and job satisfaction.

Challenges and Growth: Restlessness can be a challenge for Sagittarian workers, as they may find it difficult to stay engaged with repetitive or monotonous tasks. Offering them roles that require strategic thinking, travel, or learning opportunities can help keep them motivated and committed.

THE SAGITTARIAN BUSINESS PARTNER

The Adventurous Entrepreneur

Partnership Dynamics: Sagittarian business partners are adventurous, optimistic, and always on the lookout for new opportunities. They bring a unique blend of enthusiasm and strategic thinking to partnerships, driven by a desire for growth and expansion. Their ability to envision future possibilities makes them excellent strategists and innovators.

Fostering Mutual Growth: Sagittarians value partnerships that are built on mutual respect and shared visions for the future. They seek business partners who are not only collaborators but also fellow adventurers, willing to take calculated risks and explore new territories together.

Challenges and Growth: Their love for freedom and disdain for micromanagement can sometimes make it challenging to deal with the day-to-day realities of running a business. Cultivating open communication and establishing clear roles and responsibilities can help maintain a healthy and productive partnership.

In each role—whether as a boss, a worker, or a business partner—Sagittarians bring their trademark enthusiasm, optimism, and love for adventure. By embracing these qualities and addressing the challenges unique to their spirited approach, Sagittarians can thrive in the professional world, turning their visionary ideas into reality and inspiring those around them to reach for the stars.

CONCLUSION

As we reach the conclusion of our journey through the expansive world of Sagittarius, "The Archer's Quest," we are reminded of the profound impact this zodiac sign has on our collective and individual pursuits of knowledge, truth, and meaning. Sagittarius embodies the joy of exploration, the unquenchable thirst for understanding the mysteries of life, and the relentless pursuit of personal and spiritual growth.

The Joy of Exploration

Sagittarius teaches us that life is an endless adventure, one that is fueled by curiosity, optimism, and the desire to experience all that the world has to offer. This sign's innate love for exploration—whether it's through physical travel, intellectual pursuits, or spiritual seeking—reminds us of the richness and diversity of the human experience. Sagittarians' journey is a testament to the idea that the pursuit of knowledge and the quest for meaning are not just noble endeavors but are essential to our growth and happiness.

The Importance of Freedom

If there's one value that Sagittarius holds above all others, it's freedom. The freedom to think, to question, to explore, and to be authentically oneself. Sagittarians inspire us to break free from the shackles of convention, to venture beyond our comfort zones, and to embrace the unknown with open arms. Their lives exemplify the truth that real growth and understanding come from the courage to pursue our paths, even when they lead us into uncharted territories.

The Quest for Truth

At the heart of every Sagittarian's journey is a quest for truth—a truth that is deep, universal, and often elusive. Sagittarius challenges us to look beyond the superficial, to question the status quo, and to seek answers that resonate with the core of our being. Their philosophical nature and ethical compass guide them in navigating the complexities of life, always with an eye toward greater understanding and ethical integrity.

The Significance of Relationships

While Sagittarians treasure their independence, their journeys are enriched by the relationships they forge along the way. The connections they make—rooted in honesty, shared adventures, and mutual respect—remind us that while the quest for knowledge and meaning is deeply personal, it is also a journey that is made richer by the companions we choose. These relationships, based on a foundation of freedom and mutual growth, are the mirrors in which Sagittarians see their reflections and the catalysts for their transformation.

In reflecting on the journey of Sagittarius, we are invited to embrace our own quests for knowledge, meaning, and truth with the same boundless enthusiasm and fearless spirit. Sagittarius's story is a beacon of light, guiding us toward a life of exploration, freedom, and the relentless pursuit of what makes life truly worth living. Let us carry forward the lessons of Sagittarius, remembering that the journey itself is as significant as the destination, and that in the vast expanse of the unknown lies the greatest potential for discovery, growth, and joy.

APPENDICES

Glossary of Astrological Terms

- **Astrology:** The study of the movements and relative positions of celestial bodies interpreted as influencing human affairs and natural phenomena.
- **Sagittarius:** The ninth sign of the zodiac, symbolized by the Archer, known for its love of freedom, exploration, and quest for knowledge.
- **Jupiter:** The ruling planet of Sagittarius, associated with growth, expansion, prosperity, and the principle of increase.
- **Zodiac:** An imaginary belt in the sky through which the sun, moon, and planets move, divided into twelve equal parts, each named after the constellation that appears in that sector.
- **Fire Sign:** One of the four elemental groups in astrology, which also includes Aries and Leo. Fire signs are known for their energetic, dynamic, and enthusiastic nature.
- **Transit:** The movement of a planet through the zodiac and its interaction with a person's natal chart, influencing current events and personal developments.
- **Natal Chart:** Also known as a birth chart, it's a map of where all the celestial bodies were in their journey around the Sun, from Earth's perspective, at the exact moment of an individual's birth.
- **Mutable Sign:** One of the three quality modes in astrology, alongside cardinal and fixed signs. Mutable signs (Gemini, Virgo, Sagittarius, and Pisces) are associated with adaptability, flexibility, and change.

EPILOGUE

As we close the pages on our exploration of Sagittarius, "The Archer's Quest," we are left with a deeper appreciation for the journey itself—the unending pursuit of knowledge, the quest for truth, and the joy found in the freedom to explore. Sagittarius, guided by the expansive energy of Jupiter, reminds us that our lives are vast canvases waiting to be filled with the vibrant colors of our experiences, dreams, and discoveries.

In Sagittarius, we find a spirit that is unbreakable, a mind that is ever-curious, and a heart that yearns for adventure. This sign teaches us the value of looking beyond the horizon, of dreaming big, and of embracing the unknown with open arms. It speaks to the wanderer in each of us, urging us to break free from the constraints of the ordinary and to embark on our own quests for meaning and fulfillment.

The stories of notable Sagittarians, their adventurous spirit, and their contributions to the world serve as beacons of inspiration, showing us the heights that can be reached when we dare to follow our passions and remain true to ourselves. They remind us that while the destination may be the goal, it is the journey—with its challenges, detours, and unexpected joys—that shapes us, teaches us, and ultimately, enriches our lives.

As we bid farewell to Sagittarius, we carry with us the lessons of the Archer: to live with optimism, to seek wisdom in all corners of the world, and to cherish the freedom to chart our own paths. May we all embrace the Sagittarian spirit within us, viewing each new day as an opportunity for adventure, learning, and self-discovery.

Let the quest never end, for it is in the seeking that we find ourselves, and it is in the journey that life's most profound truths are revealed. Here's to the adventurers, the philosophers, the seekers of truth—may your paths be wide, your spirits high, and your hearts forever open to the infinite possibilities that await.

SAGITTARIUS THEMED QUIZ

Test your knowledge of the adventurous and philosophical world of Sagittarius with this engaging quiz. See how well you understand the traits, preferences, and influences that define those born under the sign of the Archer.

Questions:
1. What element is Sagittarius associated with?
    a. A) Water
    b. B) Earth
    c. C) Air
    d. D) Fire
2. Which planet rules Sagittarius, enhancing its love for adventure and quest for knowledge?
    a. A) Mars
    b. B) Venus
    c. C) Jupiter
    d. D) Saturn
3. Sagittarius is symbolized by which figure?
    a. A) The Bull
    b. B) The Scales
    c. C) The Archer
    d. D) The Fish
4. Which of these traits is NOT typically associated with Sagittarians?
    a. A) Optimism
    b. B) Pessimism
    c. C) Adventurous
    d. D) Philosophical
5. What is a key Sagittarian desire in relationships?
    a. A) Routine and predictability
    b. B) Shared adventures and growth

c. C) Solitude and independence
   d. D) Conflict and drama
6. Sagittarius's lucky day of the week is:
   a. A) Monday
   b. B) Thursday
   c. C) Saturday
   d. D) Sunday
7. Which quality mode does Sagittarius belong to?
   a. A) Cardinal
   b. B) Fixed
   c. C) Mutable
   d. D) Stationary
8. Sagittarius is most compatible with which sign?
   a. A) Taurus
   b. B) Cancer
   c. C) Leo
   d. D) Capricorn
9. What area of life does Sagittarius often excel in?
   a. A) Following strict routines
   b. B) Pursuing higher education and travel
   c. C) Avoiding change
   d. D) Staying in one place
10. Which gemstone is considered lucky for Sagittarius?
    a. A) Ruby
    b. B) Turquoise
    c. C) Emerald
    d. D) Sapphire

Sagittarius Answers

1. D) Fire - Sagittarius is a fire sign, known for its energy, enthusiasm, and adventurous spirit.
2. C) Jupiter - Jupiter, the planet of expansion and wisdom, rules Sagittarius, enhancing its love for adventure and quest for knowledge.

SAGITTARIUS: (NOVEMBER 22 - DECEMBER 21)

3. C) The Archer - Sagittarius is symbolized by the Archer, representing the sign's aim for higher truth and exploration.
4. B) Pessimism - Optimism is a hallmark of Sagittarius, making pessimism the trait not typically associated with them.
5. B) Shared adventures and growth - Sagittarians desire relationships that include shared adventures and mutual growth.
6. B) Thursday - Thursday, ruled by Jupiter, is considered Sagittarius's lucky day.
7. C) Mutable - Sagittarius is a mutable sign, indicating adaptability and flexibility.
8. C) Leo - Sagittarius is most compatible with other fire signs like Leo, sharing a love for adventure and enthusiasm for life.
9. B) Pursuing higher education and travel - Sagittarians excel in areas that allow them to expand their horizons, such as education and travel.
10. B) Turquoise - Turquoise is considered lucky for Sagittarius, believed to bring protection and good fortune.

This quiz not only tests your knowledge about Sagittarius but also reflects the adventurous, optimistic, and philosophical nature that defines those born under this sign. Whether you're a Sagittarius or simply curious about astrology, understanding these traits can offer insights into the Sagittarian spirit and how it influences their approach to life, love, and pursuit of happiness.

DEAR SAGITTARIUS READERS,

As we reach the horizon of our journey together through "Sagittarius," I hope these pages have ignited the adventurer's spirit within you. Your sign, governed by the expansive Jupiter, is a testament to the boundless enthusiasm, the quest for wisdom, and the insatiable curiosity that propels you forward on the path of discovery.

Sagittarius, the Archer, always aiming for the stars, you are reminded that your love for exploration transcends the physical realm, venturing into the realms of the mind and spirit. You are a seeker of truths, a collector of experiences, and a guardian of freedom. This book has endeavored to mirror your journey, highlighting the joys of discovery and the richness of living a life unbound by convention.

Let this exploration be a reminder that your journey is as vast as the sky itself. Your optimistic outlook and philosophical inclinations are your compasses, guiding you through life's adventures with a hopeful heart and an open mind. Embrace your natural restlessness as a sign of your desire to grow, learn, and experience all that life has to offer.

As you continue on your path, may you carry with you the wisdom and insights gleaned from these pages. Remember, the true essence of Sagittarius lies not just in the destination but in the journey. It's in the questions asked, the paths explored, and the connections forged along the way. Your quest for knowledge and understanding is a beacon for others, inspiring those around you to embrace life's journey with the same fervor and enthusiasm.

In moments of doubt or stillness, recall the fire that

burns within you, the eternal flame of curiosity, adventure, and aspiration. Let it light your way, fueling your journey with purpose and passion. The world is vast, and the possibilities are endless for a spirit as free and boundless as yours.

So, dear Sagittarius, as this chapter concludes, know that your story is far from over. There are always new horizons to discover, new truths to uncover, and new adventures to embark upon. May your arrows fly true, may your fire never dim, and may the stars continue to guide you on your magnificent journey through life.
With admiration for your indomitable spirit and endless curiosity,

Your Guide to the Stars,

Norris Elliott

BOOKS BY THIS AUTHOR

THE POWER OF NOW: CONQUERING PROCRASTINATION

"The Power of Now: Conquering Procrastination" offers a comprehensive guide to overcoming procrastination. Written by Norris Elliott, a seasoned expert on productivity, this book is a must-read for anyone looking to achieve success and reach their full potential. Drawing from years of experience and a passion for helping others, Norris shares their insights and strategies for time management and overcoming procrastination. With practical tips and actionable advice, this book will help readers conquer their procrastination habits and unlock their full potential. Whether you're a busy professional or a student, "The Power of Now: Conquering Procrastination" will help you take control of your time, increase your productivity, and achieve your goals. Order your copy today and start your journey to a more productive, successful life.

OPEN YOUR BUSINESS: A STEP-BY-STEP GUIDE TO STARTING AND GROWING A SUCCESSFUL ENTERPRISE

"Open Your Business" is the ultimate guide for aspiring entrepreneurs looking to start and grow their own businesses.

Written by an expert in the field, this handbook is packed with practical tips, strategies, and real-world examples that will help you navigate the complex world of business ownership. From developing a business plan and securing funding to attracting and retaining staff and increasing productivity, this book covers all the essential topics you need to know to succeed. With case studies, quizzes, and a step-by-step guide, this book is the perfect tool for anyone looking to turn their business dream into reality. Whether you're just starting out or looking to take your business to the next level, "Open Your Business" is the ultimate guide to success.

WEALTH BY DESIGN: HOW TO BUILD A LIFE OF FINANCIAL FREEDOM

"Financial Literacy and Wealth Building: A Comprehensive Guide" is essential for anyone looking to take control of their financial future. Written by author Ellionaire, this book covers everything you need to know about building wealth and achieving financial freedom, including understanding financial basics, creating a budget, investing, and planning for the future. With real-world examples and practical tips, this book is a must-have for anyone looking to improve their financial literacy and achieve financial success. Whether a beginner or an experienced investor, this book will provide you with the knowledge and tools you need to reach your financial goals. With easy-to-understand language and a step-by-step approach, "Financial Literacy and Wealth Building" is the perfect guide for anyone looking to take control of their finances and build a better future.

THE ASTROLOGY OF LOVE: FIND YOUR PERFECT COMPATIBLE SOUL MATE

Discover the secrets to finding your perfect match with "The

Astrology of Love: Find Your Perfect Compatible Soulmate." This enlightening book by celebrated author Norris Elliott offers a unique blend of astrological wisdom and practical advice to guide you on your journey of love and compatibility.

Key Features:

Unlock Love's Cosmic Code: Explore how astrology can influence and guide your romantic journey, helping you find and nurture fulfilling relationships.
Zodiac Compatibility Decoded: Dive deep into the dynamics of each zodiac sign and learn how they interact in love, unveiling the path to your ideal partner.
Planetary Influences Unveiled: Understand how Venus, Mars, and the Moon shape your romantic desires, emotional needs, and relationship styles.
Real-Life Love Stories: Be inspired by real-life examples and case studies that illustrate how astrology has helped others find and sustain love.
Easy-to-Use Astrological Tools: Gain practical and easy-to-apply tools to harness the power of astrology in finding and deepening your romantic connections.
Stunning Visuals and Charts: Enjoy beautifully crafted illustrations and charts that make learning astrology both enjoyable and visually engaging.
Expert Guidance: Benefit from Norris Elliott's extensive research in astrology and relationship counseling, offering insights that are both profound and accessible.
Perfect for:

Singles searching for a meaningful and lasting relationship.
Couples seeking to deepen their understanding and connection.
Astrology enthusiasts eager to explore the romantic aspects of the zodiac.
Readers looking for a blend of entertainment, practical advice, and astrological insight.

Let "The Astrology of Love: Find Your Perfect Compatible Soulmate" be your guide in the journey of love, helping you navigate the stars to find the heart that beats in harmony with yours.

THE POWER OF THE EARTH: EARTH MEDICINE: THE HEALING POWER OF GROUNDING FOR MIND, BODY, AND SOUL

Grounding or earthing is a fascinating and natural practice involving direct physical contact with the Earth's surface. This comprehensive and engaging book explores the latest scientific research and real-world case studies to delve into the potential benefits of grounding for overall health and well-being.

From the antioxidant effect of the Earth's natural supply of electrons to the potential benefits of grounding for improved sleep, reduced pain, stress, and anxiety levels, improved cardiovascular health, and enhanced athletic performance, this book covers all aspects of grounding.

We also explore the spiritual and metaphysical dimensions of grounding, its connection to traditional healing practices and spiritual traditions worldwide, and its potential for personal growth, self-discovery, and spiritual development.

The book also discusses practical tips for helping children incorporate grounding into their daily routines, the connection between grounding and our relationship with nature, and the potential for grounding to mitigate the harmful effects of environmental toxins on the body.

In the final chapter, we explore the potential for grounding to become a mainstream health practice and the potential for new technologies and innovations to enhance the practice of grounding.

Overall, this book offers a compelling and comprehensive guide to the fascinating practice of grounding and its potential to improve overall health and well-being naturally and holistically.

JAMAICANISM: THE HEARTBEAT OF THE ISLAND

"Jamaicanism: The Heartbeat of the Island" - Discover Jamaica Like Never Before

Embark on an enthralling journey with "Jamaicanism: The Heartbeat of the Island," a book that peels back the layers of a land pulsating with life, culture, and history. This is not just a read; it's an experience that transports you to the vibrant heart of Jamaica. Feel the rhythm of the island through every page, as you uncover the essence of Jamaicanism.

Why "Jamaicanism" is a Must-Read:

Dive into the Rich Tapestry of Jamaican Culture: Explore the depths of Jamaican culture, from the soul-stirring beats of reggae to the vibrant traditions of dancehall. This book celebrates the diverse heritage that shapes the Jamaican spirit.

Uncover a Lush Historical Landscape: Journey through Jamaica's past, from the indigenous Taino people to the triumphs of independence. Witness the resilience of a nation shaped by a complex history of colonization and liberation.

Speak the Language of the Island: Delve into the world of Jamaican Patois, a language born from a melting pot of influences, encapsulating the island's unique cultural identity and history.

Savor the Flavors of Jamaican Cuisine: Embark on a culinary adventure with the tantalizing tastes of Jamaica. From spicy jerk chicken to sweet ackee and saltfish, discover recipes and stories behind the island's famous dishes.

Meet the People Who Shape Jamaica: Hear the stories of Jamaicans who've left their mark on the world. From iconic figures like Bob Marley and Usain Bolt to the everyday heroes shaping Jamaica's future.

Explore the Natural Beauty of Jamaica: From the misty Blue Mountains to the crystal-clear waters of the Caribbean Sea, experience the breathtaking landscapes that make Jamaica a paradise on earth.

Witness the Power of Social Change: Understand the contemporary challenges facing Jamaica and the inspiring initiatives driving social progress, environmental stewardship, and economic growth.

Experience the Vibrant Jamaican Festivals: Immerse yourself in the pulsating energy of Jamaican festivals, where music, dance, and heritage come alive in a spectacular display of cultural pride.

"Jamaicanism: The Heartbeat of the Island" is more than a book; it's a celebration of an island and its people. It's a journey that will captivate, educate, and inspire. Whether you're a seasoned traveler, a cultural enthusiast, or simply a lover of compelling stories, this book is your gateway to experiencing the true spirit of Jamaica.

Grab your copy today and let the rhythms of Jamaica move you!

PUTTING DOWN THE BULLY: FINALLY!

"Bullying is a pervasive problem that affects individuals of all ages and can devastate mental and physical health. In "Standing Up Against Bullying," "Putting Down The Bully" examines the various forms of bullying and its impacts. Through practical tips and coping strategies, readers will learn how to deal with bullying, seek help and support, and take action to overcome bullying. The author also highlights the role of bystanders and the importance of speaking up and taking a stand. With personal stories from those who have overcome bullying and a focus on hope and resilience, this book offers a comprehensive guide for anyone looking to make a difference and reclaim a sense of control and empowerment."

EMPOWERING WOMEN: OVERCOMING MARGINALIZATION

This book comprehensively examines women's marginalization, exploring the root causes and how media, technology, globalization, economic policies, governments, civil society, men and boys, and data and research all play a role. The author, who has a construction engineering and management background, wrote this book responding to a friend's fear of publishing her similar study on the topic. Through insightful analysis and real-world examples, this book offers a call to action for continued progress toward gender equality and eliminating women's marginalization—a must-read for anyone seeking to understand the complex issues facing women worldwide today.

HOW TO BE HAPPY: THE SECRET TO FINDING HAPPINESS

Looking for a guide to cultivating happiness and finding meaning in life? Look no further than this insightful and inspiring book! Drawing on the latest scientific research, personal stories and experiences, and practical tips and techniques, this book will help you cultivate happiness and find fulfillment in all aspects of your life. Whether you are looking to improve your relationships, find success and meaning at work, or simply find peace and contentment, this book will provide you with the tools and guidance you need to achieve your goals. So why wait? Start your journey to happiness and fulfillment today!

THE CONFIDENT MAN: THE ART OF SELF-ASSURANCE AND MAGNETISM

The Confident Man: The Art of Self-Assurance and Magnetism is a comprehensive guide to help men develop a confident and charismatic persona. Through insightful theory and practical exercises, the author provides readers with the tools and techniques needed to build self-confidence and improve their communication skills. This book is written by Norris Elliott, an expert in the field of self-improvement and personal development. The book covers critical topics such as developing a solid mindset, enhancing body language, improving communication skills, building self-awareness, and putting it all together. With real-world case studies, personal anecdotes, and expert insights, this book offers a unique and practical approach to self-assurance and magnetism. Whether you're looking to improve your personal or professional life, The Confident Man is the perfect guide to help you achieve your goals. So why wait? Start your journey to becoming a confident and charismatic man today!.
With clear, concise instructions and practical advice, "My Perfect Wedding" will help you plan a wedding that reflects your style and unique vision. Whether starting from scratch or just needing inspiration, this book is a must-have for every bride-to-be."

This comprehensive guide offers everything you need to plan your perfect wedding from start to finish.

LOVE TRIANGLE: THE PERFECT PLAN. A

ROMANTIC COMEDY.

Emma had always been a type-A planner. She was the kind of kid who color-coded her crayon box and had a five-year plan for her Barbies. As an adult, she turned her love for organization into a successful event-planning business. She was like a human version of Google Calendar - always on top of everyone's schedule and ensuring every detail was in its place.

Emma's latest project was her own wedding. She had meticulously planned every detail, from the seating chart to the number of sprinkles on the cake. She even had a backup plan for the backup plan. This was going to be the perfect wedding, damn it.

Enter Olivia, Emma's business partner and the Robin to her Batman. Olivia had some big news - she was pregnant and wouldn't be able to help with the wedding. Emma's reaction was somewhere between "Oh my god, congratulations!" and "Oh my god, what are we going to do?!"

As Emma was having a meltdown, an old friend named Max called. He was in town for a wedding but had missed his flight and needed a place to crash. Emma reluctantly agreed to let him stay with her, hoping he wouldn't mess up her perfectly planned life.

Max was like a walking hurricane. He was spontaneous, carefree, and the kind of guy who would jump out of a plane without checking to see if his parachute was attached. Emma was equal parts fascinated and terrified by him.

THE BAKING BOOK: CAKES, PIES, TARTS, BREAD, PUDDINGS, BARS, AND COOKIES, COOKING

The Baking Book; Cakes, Pies, Tarts, Bread, Puddings, bars, and Cookies, Cooking is the ultimate guide to help you master the art of baking. This comprehensive book covers everything from cakes, pastries, and pies to loaves of bread and puddings. You'll learn about essential baking equipment, ingredients, schedules, conversions, and history. Whether you're a novice or an experienced baker, this book is packed with tips and tricks, troubleshooting guides, and much more. Discover the science behind baking and how to perfect your techniques for consistent results every time. With easy-to-follow recipes and step-by-step instructions, you'll be able to create delicious baked goods that everyone will love. So why wait? Start baking with confidence and make it happen with The Baking Book. Baking, Cakes, Pastries, Pies, Bread, Puddings, Baking Equipment, Ingredients, Baking Schedules, Conversions, History, Tips, Tricks, and Troubleshooting.

SEDUCER: THE ART OF SEDUCTION

Unleash the Art of Seduction with this comprehensive guide! Discover the secrets of captivating and satisfying relationships through a blend of mindfulness, cultural awareness, and sexual technique. This book guides you on a journey of self-discovery, helping you develop a more intentional approach to your relationships and interactions. With tips and advice for navigating every stage of a relationship, this book is a must-read for anyone looking to spice up their love life. Get your copy today and start your seductive journey!

BE A CONFIDENT WOMAN: HOW TO GAIN CONFIDENCE

If you want to boost your self-confidence, improve your

communication skills, and build a more charismatic persona, then Be A Confident Woman: How To Gain Confidence is the perfect book for you. Written by an expert in self-improvement and personal development, this book offers a comprehensive guide to help you achieve your personal and professional goals.

BE A CONFIDENT MAN: HOW TO GAIN CONFIDENCE

Through insightful theory and practical exercises, you'll learn the tools and techniques needed to develop a solid mindset, enhance your body language, improve your communication skills, build self-awareness, and put it all together. The real-world case studies, personal anecdotes, and expert insights in this book provide a unique and practical approach to self-assurance and magnetism.

Whether you're looking to advance your career, build stronger relationships, or simply feel more confident in your daily life, The Confident Man has something to offer. So, if you're ready to start your journey towards becoming a confident and charismatic man, then this book is a must-have!

THE 3 6 9 METHOD OF MANIFESTATION: PERSONALIZED PATHS TO SUCCESS THROUGH ANCIENT WISDOM

Unlock the Secret Power of the Universe with THE 3 6 9 METHOD OF MANIFESTATION: Personalized Paths to Success Through Ancient Wisdom

☐ Discover the transformative power of Nikola Tesla's secret code —Learn how the numbers 3, 6, and 9 can unlock your potential to manifest desires.

☐ Master the Art of Manifestation—Step-by-step guidance on integrating the 3 6 9 method into your daily routine for effective manifestation.

☐ Tailor the Practice to Your Life—Personalization techniques to ensure the 3 6 9 method resonates with your unique energy and lifestyle.

☐ Navigate Life's Challenges—Practical solutions for overcoming skepticism, obstacles, and maintaining your commitment to your manifestation journey.

☐ Real Success Stories—Be inspired by real-life examples of individuals who have successfully used the 3 6 9 method to change their lives.

☐ Comprehensive FAQs and Resources—Your burning questions are answered, plus resources for further exploration and deepening your practice.

Whether you're a seasoned practitioner of the law of attraction or new to the concept of manifestation, this book offers a fresh perspective on how to harness universal energies to create the life you've always dreamed of. Dive deep into the mystery and mechanics of the 3 6 9 method, and embark on a journey of self-discovery, personal growth, and unimaginable success.

Start manifesting your desires with clarity, purpose, and a newfound understanding of the universe's profound wisdom. Your journey to a more fulfilled life begins here.

THE LIVE SOCIAL MEDIA STREAMING BIBLE:

HOW TO DOMINATE THE LIVE STREAMING WORLD: A SIMPLE GET TO THE POINT GUIDE TO MAKE YOU FAMOUS AND RICH

"Unleash the power of live streaming with 'THE LIVE SOCIAL MEDIA STREAMING BIBLE.' This comprehensive guide is your key to building a successful career in the digital age. From setting up your stream to engaging your audience, monetizing your content to navigating legal and ethical considerations, this book covers it all. With practical tips, expert insights, and real-life case studies, you'll learn how to create compelling content, grow your audience, and turn your passion into a profitable career. Whether you're a seasoned streamer or just starting, 'THE LIVE SOCIAL MEDIA STREAMING BIBLE' is your ultimate resource for success in the world of live streaming. Get your copy today and take your streaming game to the next level!"

- [ ] Setting up your stream
- [ ] Engaging your audience
- [ ] Monetizing your content
- [ ] Navigating legal and ethical considerations
- [ ] Practical tips and expert insights
- [ ] Real-life case studies
- [ ] Creating compelling content
- [ ] Growing your audience
- [ ] Turning your passion into a profitable career
- [ ] Ultimate resource for success in the world of live-streaming

BBL: EVERYTHING YOU SHOULD KNOW BEFORE, DURING AND AFTER

Embark on a transformative journey with "Brazilian Butt Lifts Everything You Should Know Before, During and After" and unlock the secrets to achieving your dream silhouette!

☐ Comprehensive Insights: Dive into a wealth of knowledge, from pre-surgery considerations to post-op care, all crafted by top industry experts.

☐ Real-Life Transformations: Be inspired by genuine stories, rich in detail and emotion, guiding you through real experiences.

☐ Safety as Priority: Navigate the complexities of cosmetic procedures with our in-depth safety guides and surgeon selection tips.

☐ Innovation at Your Fingertips: Stay ahead with the latest trends and technological advancements in the field.

Elevate your journey from aspiration to reality. This guide isn't just a book; it's your partner in achieving the confidence and curves you've always desired!

Disclaimer

This book is intended for informational and educational purposes only. The views, thoughts, and opinions expressed herein belong solely to the author(s) and contributors. While every effort has been made to ensure the accuracy and completeness of the information contained in this book, the author(s) and publisher make no guarantee and accept no responsibility or liability for errors or omissions for the content provided or for any loss or damage caused by the use of the information provided.

This book does not offer medical, legal, psychological, or any other professional advice. If professional assistance is required, the services of a competent professional should be sought. The strategies and suggestions contained in this book may not be suitable for every individual and are not guaranteed or warranted to produce any particular outcome. The case studies and scenarios presented are provided for illustrative purposes only and may not reflect actual individuals or events.

The author(s) and publisher disclaim any liability, loss, or risk, personal or otherwise, which is incurred as a consequence, directly or indirectly, of the use and application of any of the contents of this book. Readers should use their own judgment and consult with professionals when necessary before implementing any strategies or recommendations set forth in this book.

NOTES

NOTES

Made in the USA
Monee, IL
26 April 2024

57577605R00036